Butterfly Butterfly

Edited by Linda Meyer and Mrs. Mac

Paperback ISBN: 978-1-943241-03-3
EPUB ISBN: 978-1-943241-08-8
Mobipocket ISBN: 978-1-943241-23-1
ePDF ISBN: 978-1-943241-29-3

Library of Congress Control Number: 2015943297

Phonic Monic Books
www.phonicmonic.com

C&C Joint Printing Co. (Guangdong) Ltd.
Chunhu Industrial Eatate, Pinghu
Long Gang, Shenzhen, PRC 518111
www.candcprinting.com

First Edition – April 2016

Image Credits:
Cover; Vaclav Volrab/Shutterstock, Editor pg.; Vaclav Volrab/Shutterstock, Dedication pg.; Vaclav Volrab/Shutterstock, Pan Xunbin/Shutterstock; 1, Cathy Keifer/Shutterstock; 2, PeJo/Shutterstock; 3, Palo_ok/Shutterstock; 4, Protasov AN/Shutterstock; 5, Mathisa/Shutterstock; 6, Cathy Keifer/Shutterstock; 7, IrinaK /Shutterstock; 8, hwongcc/Shutterstock; 9, hwongcc/Shutterstock; 10, hwongcc/Shutterstock; 11, neil hardwick/Shutterstock; 12, Mathisa/Shutterstock; 13, amnachphoto/amnachphoto/Thinkstock; 14, del.Monaco/Shutterstock; 15, Jag_cz/Shutterstock; 16, Chang Ching Hwong/Shutterstock; 17, Sari ONeal/Shutterstock; 18, teptong/Shutterstock; 19, antpkr/Shutterstock; 20, Olga Bogatyrenko/Shutterstock; 21, njaj/Shutterstock; 22, Gilles San Martin under Creative Commons Attribution-Share Alike 3.0 Unported License; 23; http://commons.wikimedia.org/wiki/File:Bicyclus_anynana_egg_4.JPG, Gilles San Martin under Creative Commons Attribution-Share Alike 3.0 Unported License; 24; http://commons.wikimedia.org/wiki/File:Pararge_aegeria_egg_with_embryo.jpg, Vaclav Volrab/Shutterstock; 25, Steven RussellSmithPhotos/Shutterstock; 26, Teptong/Thinkstockphotos; 27, Vaclav Volrab/Shutterstock; 29.

This book is dedicated in memory of my dad,
-a wonderful dad.

Caterpillar, caterpillar,

Eggs in a batch.

Caterpillar, caterpillar,

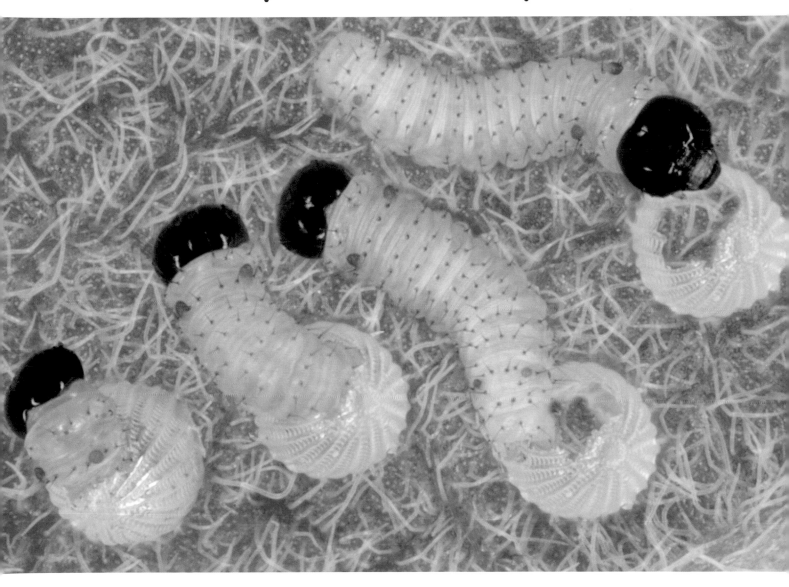

You can hatch.

Caterpillar, caterpillar,

On the ground.

Caterpillar, caterpillar,

Crawl around.

Caterpillar, caterpillar,

Eat your lunch.

Caterpillar, caterpillar,

Crunch, crunch, crunch.

Caterpillar, caterpillar,

This is it.

Caterpillar, caterpillar,

Make a chrysalis.

Caterpillar, caterpillar,

Go and hide.

Caterpillar, caterpillar,

Go inside.

Caterpillar, caterpillar,

Don't make a peep.

Caterpillar, caterpillar,

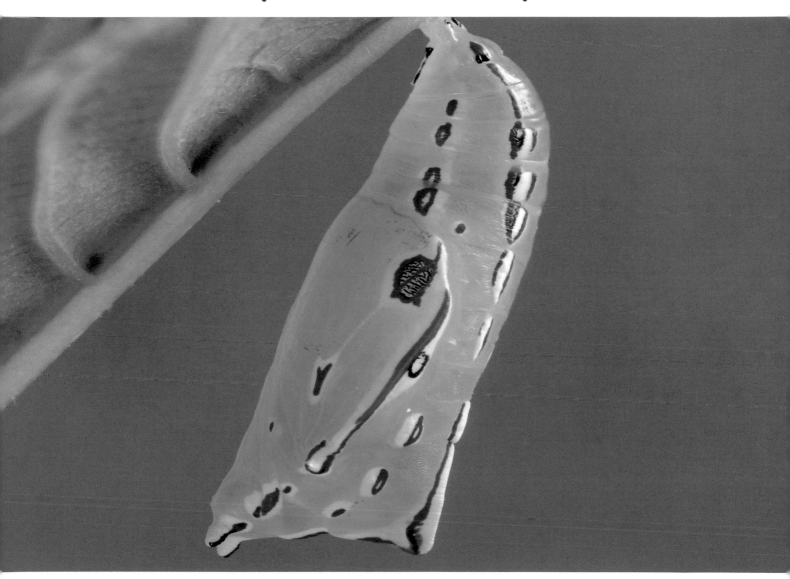

Fall into a deep, deep sleep. Zzzzzz...

Caterpillar, caterpillar,

Snug inside.

Caterpillar, caterpillar,

Metamorphosize!

Caterpillar, caterpillar,

Come out now!

Oh my! You're a butterfly!

Wow!

Butterfly, butterfly,

Do your thing.

Butterfly, butterfly,

Flap your wings.

Butterfly, butterfly,

Spend your hours.

Butterfly, butterfly,

Drink from flowers.

Butterfly, butterfly,

Straw-like mouth.

Butterfly, butterfly,

Fly down south.

Butterfly, butterfly,

Lay eggs in a batch.

Springtime, springtime,

Eggs will hatch.

Metamorphosis

Caterpillar to a Butterfly

About the Author

Cammie Ho lives with her husband and two children in California, where she studied and obtained her Elementary School Teaching Credential and her Master's Degree in Teaching English as a Second Language.

Cammie loves reading books to her children, and is inspired by her favorite children's book authors, Dr. Seuss, and Bill Martin Jr. She is developing an early learning program using music and chants to teach young children, believing that children learn well through a variety of fun channels. She writes lyrics and produces songs that teach reading and spelling in a program called, Phonic Monic.

www.phonicmonic.com